# MORE
# PRAYERS AND GRACES

*a second book of unusual piety*

collected by
## ALLAN M. LAING

with illustrations by
## MERVYN PEAKE

LONDON
VICTOR GOLLANCZ LTD
1957

# ACKNOWLEDGMENTS

KIND PERMISSION FOR the use of copyright material (for which I am duly grateful) has been granted by Messrs. George Allen & Unwin, Ltd. (for J. M. Synge's poem, *The Curse*); Messrs. Jonathan Cape, Ltd. and the Exors. of Samuel Butler (for a prayer from *Samuel Butler's Notebooks*); Messrs. Robert Hale, Ltd. (for a passage from Fred Gresswell's *Bright Boots*); and "Harley Quinn" (for the *Prayer of a Property Profiteer*). In several cases I have been unable to make contact with copyright owners, and I hope they will forgive me for taking permission for granted.

I take the opportunity here to thank correspondents who, after the publication of *Prayers and Graces* (this little book's predecessor), very kindly sent me further examples of "extraordinary piety"; and I much regret my inability to include more than a few of them herein.

A. M. L.

# A CHILD'S PRAYER

Make me, dear Lord, polite and kind
   To everyone, I pray;
And may I ask you how you find
   Yourself, dear Lord, today?

JOHN BANNISTER TABB.

# CONTENTS

## A GRUMBLING GRACE

WHEN YOU GOT to the table you couldn't go right to eating, but you had to wait for the widow to tuck down her head and grumble a little over the victuals, though there warn't really anything the matter with them.

MARK TWAIN (*Huckleberry Finn*).

## SKY PILOT PETITIONED

THE HEARTFELT prayer of a little London girl when she heard a flying-bomb was: "O God, give it strength to go on!"

# PRAYER OF A POOR PEDESTRIAN

O GOD, who filled all heaven with stars
And then all earth with motor cars,
    Make room within thy cosmic plan
    For me, a poor pedestrian.

Spread Thou before me, I entreat,
A threadlike pathway for my feet;
    And do Thou watch me lest I stray
    From this, Thy strait and narrow way.

Give me an ear alert, acute,
For each swift car's peremptory hoot:
    Teach me to judge its headlong pace
    And dodge it with a nimble grace.

When drivers' looks and words are black,
Restrain me, Lord, from answering back:
    O bless me with a nature meek
    To bear with smiles each narrow squeak.

And if one day Thy watchful eye
Should be withdrawn, and I should die,
    One boon I crave, upon my knees:
    Exonerate the driver, please.

A. M. L.

## A BULLETIN FOR GOD

WE THANK Thee, O God, that our friend Joshua Wilkinson is able to sit up and eat a little dry toast. . . .

*From a Prayer in a Friends' Meeting House.*

## PIETY AND TURPENTINE

THE FOLLOWING petition was sent up by the Rev. Jim McCoy at a prayer meeting in a Georgia turpentine camp:

"O, Lawd, give Thy servant dis mawnin' de eyes ob de eagle an' de wisdom ob de owl; connect his soul wid de gospel telephone in de central skies; 'luminate his brow wid de sun ob Heaven; turpentine his imagination; grease his lips wid possum oil; loosen his tongue wid de sledge-hammer ob Thy power; 'lectrify his brain wid de lightnin' ob Thy word; put 'petual motion in his arms; fill him plum full ob de dynamite ob Thy glory; 'noint him all over wid de kerosene ob Thy salvation; and then, deah Lawd, set him on fire."

## A PUZZLE FOR OMNIPOTENCE

... AND BE Thou with us and comfort us, O Lord, through eternity—and beyond.

## NO VICTORY, NO PRAISE

WEE DESIRE THE Corant-makers to be inspired with the spirit of truth, that one may know when to praise Thy blessed and glorious name and when to pray unto Thee; for we often praise and Laude Thy Holy Name for the King of Sweden's victories and afterwards we heare that there is noe such thing, and we oftentime pray unto Thee to relieve the same King in his distresses, and we Likewise heare that there is noe such Cause.

*Prayer offered at the University of Oxford during the reign of Charles I.*

# A RITUAL COMMENTARY

The Duke of Cambridge, George IV's younger brother, had an amusing, if reprehensible habit of making his own responses to the service in church, aloud. "Let us pray," said the clergyman. "By all means," responded the Duke. On suitable occasions the clergyman would pray for rain. "No good," announced the Duke, after one such prayer, "so long as the wind is in the east."

# THE LORD AS LAND AGENT

O Lord, Thou knowest that I have nine houses in the city of London, and that I have lately purchased an estate in fee simple in Essex. I beseech Thee to preserve the two counties of Middlesex and Essex from fires and earthquakes. And, as I have also a mortgage in Hertfordshire, I beg Thee also to have an eye of compassion on that county, and for the rest of the counties Thou mayest deal with them as Thou are pleased. O Lord, enable the Banks to answer all their bills, and make all debtors good men. Give prosperous voyage and safe return to the Mermaid sloop because I have not insured it. And because Thou hast said: "The days of the wicked are but short," I trust that Thou wilt not forget Thy promise, as I have an estate in reversion on the death of the profligate young man, Sir J. L. . . . Keep my friends from sinking, preserve me from thieves and housebreakers, and make all my servants so honest and faithful that they may always attend to my interests, and never cheat me out of my property night or day.

*Composed by* JOHN WARD, M.P., *in 1727.*

## GOD AND THE PERCYS

A WIT WHO WAS staying with the Percys found, when he attended chapel, that the place was so full of Percy pews, Percy memorials and so forth, that he wondered the parson did not begin the service with "Almighty and most Percyful God."

## THE LORD'S BUSINESS

*(Sir Jacob Astley prays before the Battle of Edgehill)*

"O LORD, THOU knowest how busy we must be today: if we forget Thee, do not Thou forget us. For Christ's sake. Amen."

# A COMMINATORY EXERCISE

*(To a sister of an enemy of the author's, who disapproved
of "The Playboy of the Western World.")*

LORD, CONFOUND this surly sister,
Blight her brow with blotch and blister:
Cramp her larynx, lung and liver:
In her guts a galling give her.

Let her live to eat her dinners
In Mountjoy with seedy sinners:
Lord, this judgment quickly bring,
And I'm your servant, J. M. Synge.

JOHN MILLINGTON SYNGE.

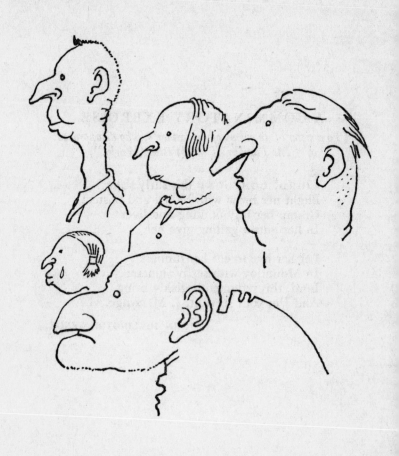

## A PRAYER FOR ENDURANCE

LORD, ON WHOM all love depends,
Let me make and keep good friends:
Bless me, also, with the patience
To endure my wife's relations.

## AMBIGUOUS THANKS

THE USUAL, drastically brief, naval grace is "Thank God." An admiral, entering late for dinner, looked round the dining-table and said: "No chaplain? Thank God."

## NUDGING THE LORD

IN ONE OF THE older Sunday schools, attended by crowds of unruly boys, the Superintendent once prayed:

"O Lord, Jimmy Wilson is leaning head downwards over a form at the back of the room. Grant that he may not fall over and break his neck."


## CHROMATIC METABOLISM

On CHINA BLUE my lobster red
    Precedes my cutlet brown,
With which my salad green is sped
    With yellow Chablis down.

Lord, if good living be no sin,
    But innocent delight,
O polarize these hues within
    To one eupeptic white!

SIR STEPHEN GASELEE.

# RELATIVITY

A PRAYER OF the minister of the Cumbrays, two miserable islands in the mouth of the Clyde: "O Lord, bless and be gracious to the Greater and the Lesser Cumbrays and in thy mercy do not forget the adjacent islands of Great Britain and Ireland."

*From the* DIARY OF SIR WALTER SCOTT.

## PIOUS BUT PIGHEADED

GRANT, O GOD, that we may always be right, for Thou knowest we will never change our minds.

OLD SCOTTISH PRAYER.

## PETITION FROM SAMUEL BUTLER

SEARCHER OF SOULS, You who in heaven abide,
To whom the secrets of all hearts are open,
Though I do lie to all the world beside,
From me to these no falsehoods shall be spoken.
Cleanse me not, Lord, I say, from secret sin
But from those faults which he who runs can see.
'Tis these that torture me, O Lord, begin
With these and let the hidden vices be;
If You must cleanse these too, at any rate
Deal with the seen sins first, 'tis only reason,
They being so gross, to let the others wait
The leisure of some more convenient season;
    And cleanse not all even then, leave me a few,
    I would not be—not quite—so pure as You.

*From the notebooks of* SAMUEL BUTLER.

# IT'S THE INTENTION THAT COUNTS

Little Elsie having been told that Grandma, who was unwell, would be better when the warm weather came, prayed: "God bless Mummy and Daddy, and make it hot for Grandma."

# SPOONERIAN WISDOM

THE AGED AND devout rector of a Warwickshire village, wiser than he intended, prayed for "that world which the peace cannot give."

## A LAST RESOURCE

MRS. KENDAL, the famous actress, once said to her stage manager: "Bring a kitchen chair and set it in the middle of the stage." She then called for the company and when the company was assembled, she knelt down and prayed: "O Lord, we pray Thee that out of Thy infinite mercy Thou wilt cause some notion of the rudiments of acting to be vouchsafed to this company, for Jesus Christ's sake. Amen." She then got up, dusted her knees and said: *"Well, now, we'll see what that will do!"*

# YOU'RE TELLING HIM!

Rufus Jones, of the Society of Friends, was present once at an all-day meeting at which during the closing prayer the minister remembered the omission of several important notices. He prayed: "Thou knowest, O Lord, that there is plenty of lunch for all who may wish to stay at noon, and Thou knowest, O Lord, that there is hay in the shed behind the meeting house for all the horses."

## IN SUNDRY PLACES

THE GUEST WAS late for family prayers, and sat down as he entered, near the door, while his host prayed: "O Lord, before whom all are equal . . ." This prayer finished, and before passing to a reading from the Scriptures, the host signed to his guest to come up and, when he approached, whispered to him: "You are sitting among the servants."

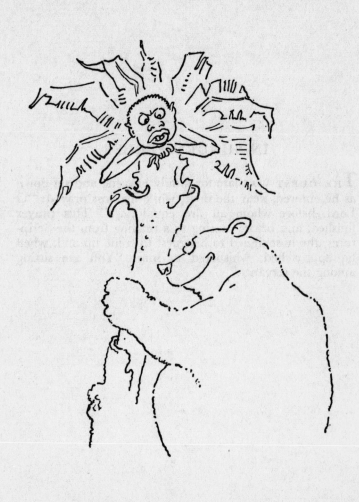

## PETITION FOR DIVINE NEUTRALITY
### (*from a Negro tree'd by a bear*)

O LAWD, EF YO' kain't help me, don't help dat b'ar.



## SURPRISING GOD

STRANGE AS IT may seem to Thee, O God . . .

*Beginning of an exordium at a Quaker meeting.*

# THE WRONG ADDRESS

"I AM GENERALLY so dead beat by the time I kneel down to pray," said the late Henry Hawkins, "that I begin out of habit: 'Gentlemen of the Jury!'"

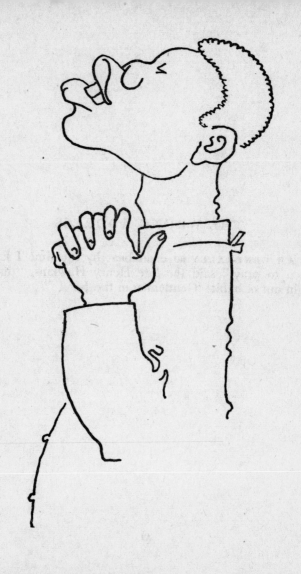

"I am somehow so constituted that I live to revolt and rebel. It may be, that I begin to realise I cannot do this alone."

## PRINCIPALS ONLY

A Negro congregation, praying to Jesus for help in lifting the debt on the church, was interrupted by the pastor, who exclaimed:

"No, Lawd, don' sen' de blessed Jesus. Come right down Yo'self. Dis ain't no boy's job."

# THREATENING THE LORD

A CERTAIN SIMPLE lay-brother in Hemmenrode was very grievously tempted; and once, as he stood in prayer, he used the following words: "Indeed, Lord, if Thou dost not deliver me from this temptation I will complain of Thee to Thy mother." The merciful Lord, who is the master of humility and the lover of simplicity, forestalled the complaint of the lay-brother, as if He feared to be accused to His mother, and immediately made his temptation easier. There was another lay-brother standing behind him at the time, and when he heard this prayer, he smiled and told it to others to edify them.

Who would not be edified by such marvellous humility of the Saviour?

CAESARIUS OF HEISTERBACH.

# NOT HEAVEN'S TARGET

Lord Londesborough, who was fond of shooting, but a very bad shot, was once heard to exclaim: "O God, You know how much I like shooting. Why won't You allow me to hit these partridges?"

# A SPORTING OFFER

THE LITTLE NEGRO boy was competing in a race, but kept dropping behind, so that, for a while, his chances of victory seemed slim. Suddenly, however, his legs began to move faster and with great regularity. He passed all his rivals and eventually won the race. Someone asked him afterwards what had happened, and why and what he had been whispering to himself as he ran. He replied that he had been praying to the Lord, saying over and over again: "Lawd, you pick 'em up an' I'll put 'em down."

# WHEN THE WORM TURNS

O, MAY THY powerful word
   Inspire the feeble worm
To rush into Thy Kingdom, Lord,
   And take it as by storm.

*From the Wesleyan Hymnbook.*

## HAPPY AMBIGUITY

AT A BROADCAST of a church service, the minister prayed: "Lord, there are those afflicted by the radio today: comfort them, we ask Thee."

## DIVINE CONSULTANT

THE DEACON OF a chapel in Yorkshire, owing to the weight of his years, had been persuaded by the brethren to retire. He agreed, but asked if he might offer a prayer before relinquishing office. He said: "O Lord, if I can no longer be a labourer in your vineyard, will You use me in an advisory capacity?"

# INCONGRUOUS ADVICE

F. H. GILLINGHAM, the old Essex cricketer, preaching a sermon in his latter days, implored the old ladies in the congregation "to keep their bats straight and get their left toe out to the pitch of the ball."

## ECSTASY OF A BISHOP

An evangelical bishop, watching a football match, sees the centre-forward slam the ball into the net. He thereupon throws his silk hat into the air, crying: "Oh, what an abundantly blessed goal!"

# THE CROFTER'S PRAYER

A CROFTER, HOLDING family prayers on a Sabbath night, offered prayer for his three sons, William, a soldier, John, in the Royal Navy, and Davie, aged seventeen, living at home and helping on the croft:

O Lord God of Battles, stretch forth Thy hand, we beseech Thee, over oor Wullie, who, as Thou art aware, is a sodger, in the Seaforth Highlanders, and is fechtin' in France. Protect him from all the perils o' the battlefield, and bring him hame safe after a victorious peace. And O Lord, Thou whose paths are in the sea, and whose ways are in the deep watters, stretch forth Thy protecting hand over oor John, a Leading Seaman in the Royal Sovereign: guard him from all the perils of the sea and guide him hame in safety unto the harbour where he would be.

An' then, Lord, there's wee Davie—ach, Lord, never fash yer thoomb aboot wee Davie. He's here at hame wi' us, and we can look after him wursels.

# PRAYER OF A PROPERTY PROFITEER

On Sunday, Lord, a Mrs. Drew
Is coming here the house to view
   Which is, of course, for sale.
Grant Thou, O Lord, that she forbear
From standing long upon the stair
   That is, alas! too frail.

O do not let her hand draw back
The curtain and reveal the crack
   Along the window-pane!
O guide her as she comes and goes,
So that no smell assails her nose
   From the adjacent drain.

Let her not see the neighouring slum
As she approaches. May she come
   Along the better road,
And grant that she may, in a trice,
Agree to the inflated price
   We ask for our abode.

And grant, O Lord, to us who plead,
These favours that we may succeed
   In what we now devise,
And through thine all-embracing love
Be made eternal tenants of
   Thy mansion in the skies.

HARLEY QUINN.

61

# THE LORD IS MISINFORMED

I OBSERVE THAT in the form of prayer for use on January 3 we are to ask forgiveness "because we have indulged in national arrogance, finding satisfaction in our power over others rather than in our ability to serve them." May I point out that this is a severe censure on all public servants in India, the Crown Colonies, and the Mandated Territories? What grounds are there for stating that this large body of public servants have grossly failed in their duty?

*From a letter to "The Times".*

# GRACE BEFORE MEAT

O LORD, WHEN hunger pinches sore,
　Do thou stand us in stead,
And send us from thy bounteous store
　A tup- or wether-head!

ROBERT BURNS.

# GRACE AFTER MEAT

LORD, THEE we thank and Thee alone,
　For temporal gifts we little merit;
At present we will ask no more—
　Let William Hislop bring the spirit.

ROBERT BURNS.

*Printed in Great Britain by*
*The Camelot Press Ltd., London and Southampton*